MiniBeasts

CHOSEN BY

Brian Moses

ILLUSTRATED BY

Jane Eccles

MACMILLAN CHILDREN'S BOOKS

For Karen and Sarah, and their inspirational snail race!

First published 1999
by Macmillan Children's Books
a division of Macmillan Publishers Ltd
25 Eccleston Place, London SW1W 9NF
Basingstoke and Oxford

Associated companies throughout the world

ISBN 0 330 37057 X

'The Vegetarian Flea' by Celia Warren was first published in *Fairground Toast and Buttered Fun* by
The Lichfield Press, 1996.

Contents

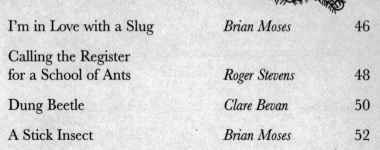

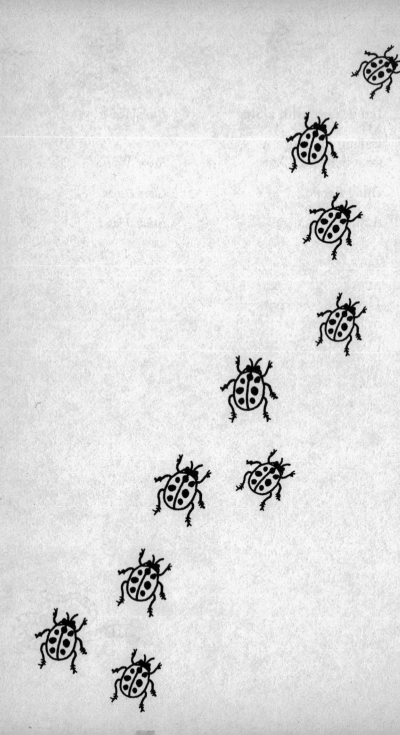

Mobile Home for Sale

Judy is a delightful
Mobile Home
with Central Heating
a warm Basement
superb Penthouse views
and includes luxury
Deep Pile Carpets
in black and white.
Fully Air-Conditioned
by large wagging tail.
This Border collie
would suit large family of fleas.

Roger Stevens

A Master of Disguise

The slick stick insect
during warm daylight hours
lies motionless;
on surveillance.
A plain-clothes detective;
a master of disguise – designed to spy,
streamlined to pry.

But as night surrounds,
he's twigged the fact that darkness
offers another form of camouflage
and is off, on the move.
Strip-searching the leaves,
rooting for information,
sticking at nothing
until his work is done.

Ian Souter

The Mayfly

A mayfly's ambition
isn't to run with the wind
or to try and get her own way.

A mayfly's ambition
is simply to be able
to live for more than one day.

Andrew Collett

Too Many Feet

I'm glad I'm not a millipede
with all those pairs of feet.
Think of all those boots to clean
before you could look neat.

And what if you had chilblains?
An itch on every toe!
Even if you scratched for hours
there'd still be some to go.

Think of wiping all those wellies
on the big mat on the floor.
Your front half would have eaten tea
before the rest came through the door!

Janis Priestley

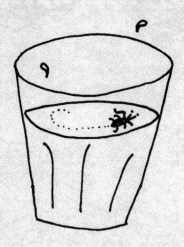

The Bug Chant

Red bugs, bed bugs,
find them on your head bugs.

Green bugs, mean bugs,
lanky, long and lean bugs.

Pink bugs, sink bugs,
swimming in your drink bugs.

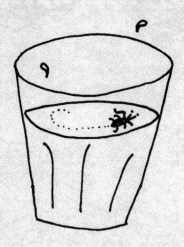

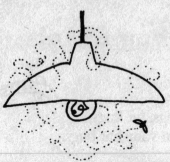

Yellow bugs, mellow bugs,
lazy little fellow bugs.

White bugs, night bugs,
buzzing round the light bugs.

Black bugs, slack bugs,
climbing up your back bugs.

Blue bugs, goo bugs,
find them in your shoe bugs.

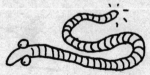

Thin bugs, fat bugs,
hiding in your hat bugs.

Big bugs, small bugs,
crawling on your wall bugs.

Smooth bugs, hairy bugs,
flying like a fairy bugs.

Garden bugs, house bugs,
lumpy little louse bugs.

Fierce bugs, tame bugs,
some without a name bugs.

Far bugs, near bugs,
'What's this over here?' bugs.

Whine bugs, drone bugs,
write some of your own bugs.

Bzzzzzzzzzzzzzzz . . .

Tony Mitton

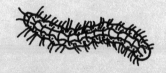

Split Personality

Patrick the worm's not his usual self,
He got chopped in two with a pick –
So his front half is now known as Pat
And his other half's now known as Rick.

Philip Waddell

Cyberspider

'Welcome to my
Website,'
said Cyberspider
to a fly.

'I've got Virtual
Reality.
Why not give
my games a try?'

Poor little fly
pressed 'ENTER.'

Cyberspider
pressed 'BYE BYE.'

Michael Johnson

13

Slugs

Slugs large, slugs small,
Slugs line-dancing on the garden wall.
Sadly Dad brings their dancing to a halt
With a sour sprinkle of savage salt.

John Kitching

The Vegetarian Flea

Mum says I should join a circus;
She thinks I'm a freak,
But just the thought of sucking blood
Makes my legs turn weak.

Once I bit a dog and it tasted awful,
Then I bit a cat and was nearly sick,
But when I bit a carrot I went back for seconds
And I took three bites from a celery stick.

Nothing tastes better than banana
And I love a bit of Stilton cheese,
But we just don't like the taste of blood,
We vegetarian fleas.

Celia Warren

I Love All Crawly Creatures

I love all crawly creatures,
 dragonflies and bees,
I love all crawly creatures
 but I can't stand bugs and fleas!

I love ladybirds and midges
 (I wash spiders down the plughole),
mayflies are fine and fireflies shine
 but ants crawl in your lughole!

I love the sounds all crawlies make,
 their buzzings, hums and throttles,
the droning round my little ears
 of squadrons of bluebottles!

John Rice

Pond-Skaters

Question:
Who goes skating in the middle of summer?
Answer:
Pond-skaters do!

Four legs
Dimple the water
Like fingertips on stretched-tight clingfilm.

Pond-skaters move in the
Blink
Of an eye.
Rowing here,
There,
Doing the breaststroke
And leaving behind ripples of amazement.

They make their jer-
ky wingless flight
Across an upside-down sky,
Where dark blue water sloshing
Against the bank like paint
Swigs the clouds around,
Dizzily.

Tight-water walkers,
They never look down
Or lose their sense of balance.

Tension?
They live on it!

Michael Lockwood

19

Early Morning Alert from a Whitefly Colony Security Guard

(The One with the Binoculars)

'Farmer on tractor,

Out for a ride . . .?

WATCH OUT, LADS –

Insecticide!'

Trevor Harvey

Totally Fearless

Hairy spider up the wall,
aren't you scared that you might fall?

Nah!
I'm cool, man, and I'm cute.
I'd spin an instant parachute.

Barry Buckingham

Cut Out for the Job

I'm a Leaf-Cutter Ant. I'm a Do-er.
Not a Curl-up-at-Home, but a Chewer.
I don't nibble ropery,
I'm into Topiary,
An art-form delicious and pure.

My jaws are a perfect device
For patterns clean-cut and precise.
This one, as you see,
Is a rather fine bee,
And here's a complete pair of mice.

I'm working on tigers today
(Though stripes can be hard to portray).
I'm honing my powers
In shadowy bowers
And weaving gold whiskers from hay.

My ambitions are lofty, it's true –
I want to create my own Zoo,
From emerald elks
To viridian whelks,
Olive chimps and a sage kangaroo.

So if your old hedge makes you rant,
Or you long for a green elephant,
Be kind to that tree –
Leave the whole thing to me,
Here's my card . . .

Capability Ant.

Clare Bevan

How to Sing a Long Song Short

Ten Bluebottles buzzing by a wall.
One flypaper –
I think that says it all.

Maureen Haselhurst

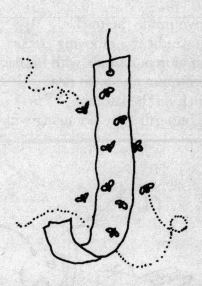

Party Time!

Down inside the thicket
you can hear a grooving cricket
twanging out a tune with his back feet
a mosquito and a cat flea
switch on the karaoke
the butterflies are bouncing with the beat.

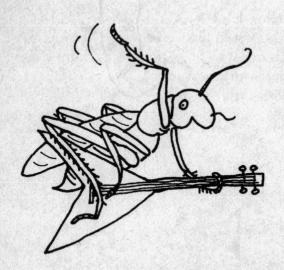

The beetle's got a band
the hottest in the land
got a bee who plays the bass with his sting
a glow-worm on guitar
a silk-worm on sitar
and a strutting spinning spider who can sing.

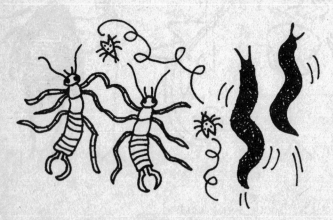

Some earwigs and some slugs
are jiving with the bugs
the gnat is rocking with the Cabbage White
whirling, leaping, hopping
bopping without stopping
the insects party on throughout the night.

When darkness turns to day
they'll creep and crawl away
without a buzz, a whisper or a squeak
but soon this woodland quiet
will be another riot
the grasshopper is twenty-one next week!

David Harmer

A DIY Poem about a Peticular Disaster

In this poem we have the following:

1. My brother
2. My brother's pet stick insects
   (which he keeps in a glass bowl)
3. My grandad
4. My mum

my brother

my brother's
pet stick insects

The following things happen, in any order:

1. Mum puts a bowl of Twiglets on the table
2. Grandad takes his glasses off
3. Grandad eats some Twiglets
4. My brother cleans out his stick insects

There is, however, a terrible mix-up.
Can you guess what it is?

my Grandad

my mum

Now, write your own poem involving all the above.
You may choose one of these lines
to end your poem if you wish:

1. Now Grandad never takes his glasses off.
2. 'Mum! Have you seen my stick insects?'
3. 'Mmmmm!' said Grandad. 'Have you any more Twiglets?'
4. My brother's stick insects never moved much after that.

Paul Cookson

Adolescent Spider

My mother dear has gone quite mad
She says I've got to leave
I treat this web like a hotel
I never sit and weave.

My mother says I stretch a point
Until it breaks the silk
And if I don't improve my ways
I'll live on bread and milk!

She says that my existence here
Is hanging by a thread
And if I don't improve my ways
I might just end up dead!

I've made a pretty tangled web
With all the lies I tell
And if I don't improve my ways
I'll go to Spider Hell!

Sally Turner

The Bedbugs are Throwing a Party

The bedbugs are throwing a party
And I know who they're going to invite.
So select your best pyjamas
And arrange to stay the night.

You'll be their guest of honour.
The cause of great delight.
If you grace them with your presence
Everything will be just right.

Do accept their invitation
(To refuse would be impolite).
And please be there for the midnight feast –
It's you they're intending to bite!

Bernard Young

WOrmhOles in Space

Intergalactic, Outerspace EarthwOrms,
flying the cOsmOs:
                    fantastic!

FrOm red stars tO white stars,
frOm planets tO mOOns
they zap,
                    with the snap! Of elastic

Intergalactic, Outerspace EarthwOrms,
but aren't they a little absurd?

NO,
they just need tO escape

 – thrOugh wOrmhOles in space –
frOm thOse ravenOus early birds.

Michael Johnson

The Ladybird Designers

Morning-wear, evening-wear,
To keep you cool or hot,
We'll design you anything
So long as it has spots.
We're the Ladybird Designers
'Tailor-made' or 'Off the Shelf'
Satisfaction guaranteed
By Lady Bird herself.
She oversees the business,
Adding glamour to each day
As she floats about the workshop
In her scarlet negligee.
Choose your style, choose your silk,
Chiffon or even plastic,

Yellow, red or subtle brown
We'll make you look fantastic.
And when you have decided
How many spots to try,
We'll dress you up and push you off,
We know you'll want to fly!
For we're the Ladybird Designers,
Quite the top of our profession,
And ruthless to our rivals,
'Aphid House' and 'Greenfly Mansion'.

Daphne Kitching

Persons

Said the nit teacher
to the nit pupil:
I'm afraid you must take
this letter to your mum.
You have a human
caught up in your feet.

Roger Stevens

The Trial of the Black Widow

The elegant Widow arrested? The shock!
There she is now, quite demure, in the dock.
The verdict is 'Guilty.' The Judge looks severe.
The sentence? The Widow produces a tear.
'I can't overlook,' says the Judge, 'this foul crime,
and the sentence,' she adds, 'will be heavy this time
for you've come up before me not once, no, but twice,
It's agreed that you'll have to be cured of this vice.
You did *not* eat your husband. You've failed as a wife.
You're a bogus Black Widow. The sentence is Life!!!'

Marian Swinger

Mossie

Don't ya mess wi me, pal,
my aim is true.
Stiletto in the shadows
hunting for you.

Nip ya on the finger,
armpit, neck or knee;
Jag ya anywhur ah like,
ya can't stop me.

See them mobbing midgies,
gang a mugging fleas;
Na style, na class, just numbers,
there's none as brave as me.

Wasps are dumb and clumsy,
one stroke an they're dud,
they're just easily upset
but I'm out for your blood.

Sandflies are sneaky nippers –
I'm elegant and proud;
Hear me coming, human,
I'll be singing clear and loud.

I like to boast and dance around
before I get stuck in –
when you can't hear me then fear
cos I'll be sucking skin.

'Float like a butterfly,
Sting like a bee' –
man, I can do all that an more,
you've no chance against me!

Dave Calder

The Quiet Guest

Don't grouse
at the woodlouse,
as it humps
and bumps
its armour-plated house.

Use your nouse.
Your house is blessed
by this harmless pest.

Best to let
this quiet guest
rest beneath the carpet.

It might be worse –
you could be cursed
by the dreaded Deathwatch beetle.

So pray that it's only
the anxious woodlouse,
curled tight
at the slightest tremble
of a word.

And don't forget
to close your mouth
while you sleep
for woodlice often fall
from the ceiling.

Pie Corbett

I'm in Love with a Slug

I'm in love with a slug,
I really think she's neat,
right from the eyes in her antennae
down to the tips of her feet.*

Yes, I'm in love with a slug,
we meet up every night,
while she's feeding in the lettuces
I watch each tender bite.

I hold her in my hand
as she looks at me with affection.
My heart begins to sing
when faced with such perfection.

*Actually, slugs only have one 'foot', but I needed 'feet' for
the rhyme!

If I could shrink to her size
I'd accompany her as she dines,
I'd like to toast her beauty
in a range of dandelion wines.

I know that I'd be the slug
she'd fall in love with too,
and underneath the slippery moon
we'd kiss, the way slugs do!

Brian Moses

Calling the Register for a School of Ants

Arrog
Cormor
Desc
Domin
Eleg
Eleph
Ignor
Imp Ort
Inhabit
Irrit
Tri Umph
Milit
Nonchal
Toler

(Now try calling the register out loud using the ants'
surnames. Arrog Ant, Cormor Ant, etc.)

Roger Stevens

Dung Beetle

I'm the Insect
Gladiator
Born to be
An excavator.
A Super-Beetle
Tough and strong
Rolling balls of
Dung along.

Now – heaving weights
Around the Zoo
May not seem
Much fun to you,
But as for me
It's just the thing
To show the Beetle-
World I'm King.

So bring the Trophy
Carve my name
On all the Insect
Walls of Fame.
And human beings
(If you're wise)
Be thankful that
I'm not *your* size.

Clare Bevan

A Stick Insect

A stick insect
is not a thick insect,
a macho-built-like-a-brick insect,
a brawl-and-break-it-up-quick insect,
not a sleek-and-slippery-slick insect
or a hold-out-your-hand-for-a-lick insect.

No way could you say it's a cuddly pet
or a butterfly that hasn't happened yet.

And it won't come running when you call
or chase about after a ball.
And you can't take it out for a walk
or try to teach it how to talk.

It's a hey-come-and-look-at-this-quick insect,
a how-can-you-tell-if-it's-sick insect,
a don't-mistake-me-for-a-stick
        insect . . .

Brian Moses

Ridiculous Relatives
poems chosen by Paul Cookson

Auntie Betty Thinks She's Batgirl

Auntie Betty pulls her cloak on
And the mask — the one with ears.
Almost ready, check the lipstick,
Wait until the neighbours cheer.
Through the window. What a leap!
She lands right in the driver's seat.
Off she goes with style and grace
To make our world a better place.

Andrea Shavick

A selected list of poetry books available from Macmillan

The prices shown below are correct at the time of going to press. However, Macmillan Publishers reserve the right to show new retail prices on covers which may differ from those previously advertised.

The Secret Lives of Teachers	0 330 34265 7
Revealing rhymes, chosen by Brian Moses	£3.50
'Ere We Go!	0 330 32986 3
Football poems, chosen by David Orme	£2.99
Aliens Stole My Underpants	0 330 34995 3
Intergalactic poems chosen by Brian Moses	£2.99
Revenge of the Man-Eating Gerbils	0 330 35487 6
And other vile verses, chosen by David Orme	£2.99
Teachers' Pets	0 330 36868 0
Chosen by Paul Cookson	£2.99
Parent-Free Zone	0 330 34554 0
Poems about parents, chosen by Brian Moses	£2.99
I'm Telling On You	0 330 36867 2
Poems chosen by Brian Moses	£2.99

All Macmillan titles can be ordered at your local bookshop or are available by post from:

Book Service by Post
PO Box 29, Douglas, Isle of Man IM99 1BQ

Credit cards accepted. For details:
Telephone: 01624 675137
Fax: 01624 670923
E-mail: bookshop@enterprise.net

Free postage and packing in the UK.
Overseas customers: add £1 per book (paperback)
and £3 per book (hardback).